Raven Moondance (aka Shenna Benarte) has been working with Grandmother Moon for over 30 years through observation, study, teaching and ceremony. She infuses moon magic into all her teaching-- yoga, energy healing, Reiki, Feng Shui, and children's library programs. Raven shows people how the moon affects us physically and emotionally by connecting the rhythms and cycles of nature to help us feel how we are all an integral part of the oneness of life. Contact Raven at the Sacred Earth Center in Gainesville, Florida at _moondance_raven@hotmail.com_

Karen White Porter M.Ed. NBCT is an educator, author, and illustrator. Her students in Scotland, China, the USA have inspired her to write, draw and develop stories. In addition to illustrating the works of others, she is the author and illustrator of the Emotatude book series. Her recent book Emotional Mandalas artistically represents different emotions. Her earlier works each deal with a separate emotion such as fear, love, joy, grief, compassion, frustration, and anger. Contact Karen at **Everfieldpress.com**

MOON ASTROLOGY

The ever-changing, silvery moon has been a source of myth, magic and fascination since ancient times--inspiring poets and lovers, intriguing scientists, guiding farmers and earth-based cultures. It is a symbol of the Goddess, the Sacred Feminine, the receptive energy that imparts healing qualities to herbs as they grow under her cooling lunar light. The moon influences the tides and waters of the earth, the waters of our body and has an especially powerful effect on our emotions. Following Grandmother Moon's monthly cycle can help us feel more connected to nature and the energies of the cosmos and bring us more in tune with our own inner spirit.

In MOON ASTROLOGY, we follow the moon's journey through its phases and through the twelve signs of the Zodiac. Attuning to the cycles of nature aligns us to the rhythms of the cosmos and gives us a glimpse into the more mystical quality of life. All things begin, grow, mature, die, transform, and begin again in some form or another.

Each quarter or phase of the moon cycle has a different quality or energy that we can consciously work to empower ourselves to become more of an active participant in our own evolutionary process. The moon influences how life unfolds, whether we are conscious of it or not. Follow the moon—one cycle at a time—observing your life, your emotions and how life flows around you.

On a NEW MOON, both the Sun and the Moon are in the same sign of the Zodiac creating an alignment that facilitates inner focus. The New Moon initiates the first week of the moon cycle—a time to go within, nurture yourself, contemplate, dream, imagine, envision, meditate....Spend more time in silence and listen....Notice what thoughts, ideas, insights, inspirations and projects come to you. Ponder, examine, investigate, observe, and feel. Be patient, especially with yourself. Trying to push forward before the first quarter moon can sometimes be frustrating. This first week, as the moon waxes, is a time of germination deep within. Staying in the moment ALLOWS life to unfold and can help us develop a deeper sense of patience and trust that we will receive what we need when the time is right!

7 DAY NEW MOON CEREMONY

This ceremony is a concrete way to put your desires out to the Universe. Begin a day or two after   where it says "the new moon occurs, on the night you see the first sliver of the moon. Write down or visualize what you would like to manifest. Choose a candle in a color that feels right for your vision. Then every night for 7 nights (beginning with the first appearance of the new moon) burn some sage or incense if you like, light your candle and read what you wrote or visualize what you would like to see manifest in your life. You may add to your vision throughout the 7 days. On the 8th day, burn your written vision (if you wrote one) and bury the ashes in the earth along with the remainder of your candle and any ashes from the sage or incense. Release your vision to the Universe asking for this or something better and to manifest in line with the highest good for all.

NEW MOON ABUNDANCE CHECK

1) On the New Moon Day, take a check from your checkbook (or draw a paper check) andto" write your name.

2) Write "Paid in Full" on the lines for $ amount and where you would normally write in the
    Pay dollar amount
3) Sign the check "LAW OF ABUNDANCE"
4) Do not put the date on the check or a specific $ amount.
5) Place check on your alter, in a journal or in a safe place and forget about it! The
    Universe will take it from there. May the Abundance FLOW!

At the First Quarter Moon, you may notice the energy nudging you forward. Suddenly, things start to fall into place. That call you have been waiting for finally comes in. During this second week of the moon cycle, our ideas begin to grow and become more concrete. As we approach the Full Moon, we can expect more "light" to be shed on whatever it is we are working on or whatever challenges or opportunities we are moving through.

On a FULL MOON, the Sun and Moon are in opposite signs of the Zodiac creating a dynamic tension that pushes us to action. The Full Moon intensifies our intuitive and psychic abilities as well as our emotions. To maintain emotional balance and mental clarity, it is helpful to intentionally utilize the full moon's energy. Three days before the full moon we begin to feel the intensity building as we move towards the actual full moon day. Then, during the three days after the full moon day, the insights, information, and guidance received during the full moon gradually become integrated into our consciousness. For each day, there is a focus to meditate, pray or simply think upon to harness the incoming energies and maintain our center.

Day#1—Affirm your complete faith and trust in the Universe that you are being guided in all your actions and in all that you are working on

Day#2—Aspire towards positive, uplifting thoughts, words and actions

Day#3—Reaffirm your total commitment to your life path or soul purpose

Day#4—FULL MOON DAY—Open to receive on this day of greatest Light! Breathe, take in and listen! Make no impulsive decisions.

Days 5, 6, 7—Allow guidance, insights, possibilities to assimilate deeper and deeper into your consciousness each day so that important decisions can be made after the 7th day with greater clarity, understanding and awareness.

The Last Quarter Moon initiates a time to re-evaluate, revise, clean out and release. This can sometimes be a challenging time as we may be pushed to clean out, release and let go of what no longer is working in our life. In Feng Shui, when we clear the clutter, energy flows better in our home and in our life. As the moon wanes, clean out your closets and deal with any unfinished emotional issues that may surface—it is time!

As you follow the moon through its phases, observe how aspects of your life begin, grow, are tested, and then revised with each new cycle. Moving from the last day of the moon cycle into the first few days of the new cycle, notice how you feel. We are in a different place as we begin each new moon cycle, and ready for the process to begin again. Use this monthly opportunity to gain insight, to grow and to deepen your connection to Spirit and the cycles of nature.

THE MOON THROUGH THE SIGNS

Each planet and heavenly body effects some aspect of life. We know that Mercury governs the mind and logical thinking. The Moon has a powerful effect on our emotions as it moves through the 12 signs of the zodiac, spending approximately 2 to 2 1/2 days in each sign. In comparison, over the course of a year (365 days) the Sun moves through all 12 signs of the zodiac staying approximately 28 to 31 days in a particular sign. The sign through which the moon "shines" influences our emotions. If you have a difficult day or two, breathe and consciously move through your experience. Within a few days, most likely you will feel a shift in your emotional state as the moon moves into the next sign.

To follow the moon's journey through the signs, look at your calendar and find the tiny hieroglyph signifying the moon in the square for a particular day. Check to see what sign the moon is in, is going into (designated by an arrow) and when the next void of course (v/c) occurs. Record how you feel at the end of each day. Over time, you will begin to see a pattern. When the moon transits or moves through certain signs, you may feel empowered while in other signs, you may feel stressed, anxious, or more emotional than usual. Our sense of empowerment is nurtured as we uncover more about our personal connection to the moon.

To follow the moon's journey through the signs, look at your calendar and find the tiny hieroglyph signifying the moon in the square for a particular day. Check to see what sign the moon is in, is going into (designated by an arrow) and when the next void of course (v/c) occurs. Record how you feel at the end of each day. Over time, you will begin to see a pattern. When the moon transits or moves through certain signs, you may feel empowered while in other signs, you may feel stressed, anxious, or more emotional than usual. Our sense of empowerment is nurtured as we uncover more about our personal connection to the moon.

♈	♉	♊	♋	♌	♍	♎	♏	♐	♑	♒	♓
Aries	Taurus	Gemini	Cancer	Leo	Virgo	Libra	Scorpio	Sagitarious	Capricorn	Aquarius	Pisces

VOID OF COURSE MOON

The moon spends approximately 2 to 2 1/2 days in each sign. Technically, when the moon makes its last aspect to a planet in a sign, it moves void of course (v/c) which is essentially a null zone, an in-between-the-worlds, or dimensions space. It is a time to take a break from the day-to- day to assimilate and download incoming energies, insights, and experiences. It is a good time to rest, relax, meditate, spend time in nature, learn something new as we will take it in on a deeper level. We may feel sleepy, unfocused, or ungrounded during a v/c. Major changes can occur during a v/c, making it possible for something profound to shift in our awareness, consciousness or understanding that will be reflected in our personal life or in the collective as the moon's journey affects everyone!

Going back to your calendar, notice that v/c occurs every 2 or 3 days. Notice the time it occurs and how long it lasts. It ends when the moon goes into the next sign. During v/c it is not a good time to sign important papers or make a commitment. Also refrain from purchasing costly items as you may end of returning or never really using them. Similarly, when a planet goes into Retrograde, the v/c time is like a mini vacation that gives us an opportunity to assimilate incoming energies and to tap into a deeper level of understanding or insight.

January

As I envision a joyful, abundant life, the details fall into place one day at a time.

January 2021

Sunday	Monday	Tuesday	Wednesday	Thursday	Friday	Saturday
December S M T W T F S 1 2 3 4 5 6 7 8 9 10 11 12 13 14 15 16 17 18 19 20 21 22 23 24 25 26 27 28 29 30 31					1 ☽ in ♌ New Year's Day	2 ☽ v/c 5:00 pm ☽ -> ♍ 8:13pm
3 ☽ in ♍	4 ☽ v/c 4:34 pm	5 ☽ -> ♎ 12:42 am	6 ☽ in ♎	7 ☽ v/c 12:55 am ☽ -> ♏ 3:53am	8 ☽ in ♏ ☽ v/c 8:59 pm	9 ☽ -> ♐ 6:15am
10 ☽ in ♐ ☽ v/c 1:29pm	11 ☽ -> ♑ 8:30am	12 ☽ in ♑	13 New Moon 12:01am ☽ v/c 2:22am ☽ -> ♒ 11:44am	14 ☽ v/c 4:28 am ♅ SD 3:36am	15 ☽ v/c in ♒ ☽ -> ♓ 5:17 pm	16 ☽ in ♓
17 ☽ in ♓ ☽ v/c 10:44 pm	18 ☽ -> ♈ 2:07 am Martin Luther	19 ☽ in ♈ ☉ -> ♒ 3:40 pm Sun enters Aquarius	20 ☽ v/c 3:29 am ☽ -> ♉ 1:56 pm	21 ☽ in ♉	22 ☽ in ♉ ☽ v/c 4:28pm	23 ☽ -> ♊ 2:43 am
24 ☽ in ♊ 31 ☽ in ♍	25 ☽ v/c 2:17 am ☽ -> ♋ 1:52 pm	26 ☽ in ♋	27 ☽ v/c 12:55 am ☽ -> ♌ 9:54pm	28 ☽ in ♌ Full Moon 2:17 pm	29 ☽ in ♌ ☽ v/c 8:53pm	30 ☽ -> ♍ 3:02 am ☿ SR 10:51 am February S M T W T F S 1 2 3 4 5 6 7 8 9 10 11 12 13 14 15 16 17 18 19 20 21 22 23 24 25 26 27 28

February

Rise up and become the person you were meant to be.

February 2021

Sunday	Monday	Tuesday	Wednesday	Thursday	Friday	Saturday
	1 ☽ in ♍ ☽ v/c6:10 am ☽-> ♎ 6:25 am	2 ☽ in ♎ Groundhog's Day	3 ☽ v/c1:15 am ☽-> ♏ 9:14 am	◗ 4 ☽ in ♏	5 ☽ v/c4:20 am ☽-> ♐ 12:16 pm	6 ☽ in ♐
7 ☽ v/c 1:16 am ☽-> ♑ 3:52 pm	8 ☽ in ♑	9 ☽ in ♑ ☽v/c12:22 pm ☽-> ♒ 8:20 pm	10 ☽ in ♒	● 11 ☽ in ♒ New moon 2:07 pm v/c2:06 pm	12 ☽-> ♓ 2:23 am	13 ☽ in ♓
14 ☽ v/c2:29 am ☽-> ♈ 10:54 am☽	15 ☽ in ♈	16 ☽ in ♈ ☽ v/c7:17 pm ☽-> ♉ 10:12 pm	17 ☽ in ♉	Sun enters Pisces 18 ☽ in ♉ ☉-> ♓ 5:44 am	◖ 19 ☽ v/c2:28 am ☽-> ♊ 11:03 am	20 ☽ in ♊ Mercury ☿ SD 7:52 am
21 in ♊ ☽ v/c1:39 pm ☽-> ♋ 10:53 pm	22 ☽ in ♋	23 ☽ in ♋ ☽ v/c 11:54p m	24 ☽-> ♌ 7:23 am	25 ☽ in ♌	26 ☽ v/c6:32 am ☽-> ♍ 12:07 pm	○ 27 full moon 3:18am ☽ in ♍
28 ☽ in ♍ ☽ v/c10:58 am ☽-> ♎ 2:17 pm						

January

S	M	T	W	T	F	S
					1	2
3	4	5	6	7	8	9
10	11	12	13	14	15	16
17	18	19	20	21	22	23
24	25	26	27	28	29	30
31						

March

S	M	T	W	T	F	S
	1	2	3	4	5	6
7	8	9	10	11	12	13
14	15	16	17	18	19	20
21	22	23	24	25	26	27
28	29	30	31			

March

I am a unique and radiant being! All my experiences serve to create who I am today!

March 2021

	Monday	Tuesday	Wednesday	Thursday	Friday	Saturday
	1	2	3	4	5	6
February	☽ in ♎	☽ in ♎	☽ in ♏	☽ in ♏	☽ in ♐	☽ v/c 4:44am
		☽ v/c 9:09am		☽ v/c 11:09 am		☽ -> ♑ 9:20pm
		☽ -> ♏ 3:38 pm		☽ -> ♐ 5:43 pm		
	7	8	9	10	11	New Moon ● 13
☽ in ♑	☽ in ♑	☽ -> ♒ 2:41am	☽ in ♒	☽ -> ♓ 9:44am	☽ in ♓	☽ in ♓
		☽ v/c 7:52pm		☽ v/c 10:32pm		New Moon 5:22am
						☽ v/c 11:38am
						☽ -> ♈ 6:44pm
Daylight Savings 14	15	16	St Patrick's Day 17	18	19	Spring Equinox 20
☽ in ♈	☽ in ♈	☽ -> ♉ 6:56am	☽ in ♉	☽ in ♉	☽ in ♊	Sun enters Aries
	☽ v/c 11:40pm			☽ v/c 4:40pm		☽ in ♊
				☽ -> ♊ 7:47pm		☉ -> ♈ 5:37am
21	22	23	24	25	26	27
☽ v/c 8:04am	☽ in ♋	☽ in ♌	☽ v/c 9:27am	☽ in ♍	☽ in ♍	
☽ -> ♋ 6:18am			☽ -> ♍ 11:25pm		☽ v/c 7:48pm	
Full Moon ○ 28	29	30	31			
☽ -> ♎ 1:22am	☽ in ♎	☽ -> ♏ 1:33am	☽ in ♏			*April*
Full Moon 2:49pm	☽ v/c 8:08pm					

April

I am open to growing and expanding who I am in new, different, and exciting ways.

April 2021

Sunday	Monday	Tuesday	Wednesday	Thursday	Friday	Saturday
March S M T W T F S 1 2 3 4 5 6 7 8 9 10 11 12 13 14 15 16 17 18 19 20 21 22 23 24 25 26 27 28 29 30 31				1 ☽→ ♐ 1:59 am	2 ☽ in ♐	3 ☽ v/c 1:23 am ☽→ ♑ 4:13 am
◑ 4 ☽ in ♑	5 ☽ v/c 3:05 am ☽→ ♒ 9:04 am	6 ☽ in ♒	7 ☽ v/c 6:05 am ☽→ ♓ 4:30 pm	8 ☽ in ♓	9 ☽ in ♓ ☽ v/c 7:48 pm	10 ☽→ ♈ 2:11 am
New Moon ● 11 ☽ in ♈ New Moon 10:32 pm	12 ☽ v/c 8:06 am ☽→ ♉ 1:44 pm	13 ☽ in ♉	14 ☽ in ♉ ☽ v/c 8:00 pm	15 ☽ in ♊ 2:35 am	16 ☽ in ♊	17 ☽ in ♊ ☽ v/c 11:03 am ☽→ ♋ 3:25 pm
18 ☽ in ♋	Sun enters Taurus 19 ☽ in ♋ ☽ v/c 8:03 pm ☉→ ♉ 4:33pm	◐ 20 ☽ ♌ 2:11 am	21 ☽ in ♌	22 ☽ v/c 8:05 am ☽→ ♍ 9:08 am	23 ☽ in ♍	24 ☽ v/c 6:50 am ☽→ ♎ 12:06 pm
25 ☽ in ♎	Full Moon ○ 26 ☽ v/c 8:40 am ☽→ ♏ 12:18 pm Full Moon 11:38pm	27 ☽ in ♏ ♇ Pluto Retrograde	28 ☽ v/c 8:31 am ☽→ ♐ 11:42 am	29 ☽ in ♐	30 ☽ v/c 9:26 am ☽→ ♑ 12:16 pm	May S M T W T F S 1 2 3 4 5 6 7 8 9 10 11 12 13 14 15 16 17 18 19 20 21 22 23 24 25 26 27 28 29 30 31

May

May 2021

I am grateful for the beauty and abundance in my life each day.

Sunday	Monday	Tuesday	Wednesday	Thursday	Friday	Saturday
April calendar						**1** ☽ in ♑
2 ☽ in ♑ · ☽ v/c 10:30 am · ☽→ ♒ 3:31pm	**3** ☽ in ♒	**4** ☽ in ♒ · ☽ v/c 8:05 pm · ☽→ ♓ 10:08pm	Cinco de Mayo **5** ☽ in ♓	**6** ☽ in ♓	**7** v/c 3:36 am · ☽→ ♈ 7:52 am	**8** ☽ in ♈
Mother's Day **9** ☽ in ♈ · ☽ v/c 6:50 pm · ☽→ ♉ 7:46pm	**10** ☽ in ♉	New Moon ● **11** ☽ in ♉ · New Moon 3:01 pm	**12** ☽ v/c 8:23am · ☽→ ♊ 8:43am	**13** ☽ in ♊	**14** ☽ v/c 6:51 am · ☽→ ♋ 9:30pm	**15** ☽ in ♋
Peace Day **16** ☽ in ♋	**17** ☽ v/c 2:23 am · ☽→ ♌ 8:44am	**18** ☽ in ♌	**19** ☽ in ♌ · ☽ v/c 3:13 pm · ☽→ ♍ 4:59pm	Sun Enters Gemini **20** ☽ in ♍ · ☉→♊ 3:37pm	**21** ☽ in ♍ · ☽ v/c 3:56 pm · ☽→ ♎ 9:35pm	**22** ☽ in ♎
♄ Saturn Retrograde **23** ☽ in ♎ · ☽ v/c 5:36 pm · ☽→ ♏ 11:00pm	**24** ☽ in ♏	**25** ☽ in ♏ · ☽ v/c 5:20pm · ☽→ ♐ 10:39pm	Full Moon ○ **26** Lunar Eclipse 7:15am · ☽ in ♐	**27** ☽ in ♐ · ☽ v/c 1:35 pm · ☽→ ♑ 10:23pm	**28** ☽ in ♑	Mercury Retrograde **29** ☽ in ♑ · ☽ v/c 6:15 pm · ☿℞ 6:34pm
30 ☽→ ♒ 12:04am	**31** ☽ in ♒					June calendar

June

My thoughts and imagination ignite sparks that create my unfolding life.

June 2021

Sunday	Monday	Tuesday	Wednesday	Thursday	Friday	Saturday
May S M T W T F S 1 2 3 4 5 6 7 8 9 10 11 12 13 14 15 16 17 18 19 20 21 22 23 24 25 26 27 28 29 30 31		1 ☽ v/c 2:14 am ☽→ ♓ 5:07 am	◑2 ☽→ ♓	3 ☽ v/c 7:10 am ☽→ ♈ 1:15 pm	4 ☽ in ♈	☽ in ♈ 5 ☽ v/c 6:47 pm
6 ☽→ ♉ 1:46 am	7 ☽ in ♉	8 ☽ in ♉ ☽ v/c 11:07 am ☽→ ♊ 2:47 pm	9 ☽ in ♊	New Moon ●10 Solar Eclipse 6::54am ☽ in ♊ ☽ v/c 1:38 pm	11 ☽→ ♋ 3:22 am	12 ☽ in ♋
13 ☽ v/c 7:16 am ☽→ ♌ 2:22 pm	14 ☽ in ♌	15 ☽ in ♌ ☽ v/c 1:27pm ☽→ ♍ 11:02 pm	16 ☽ in ♍	17 ☽ in ♍ ☽ v/c 11:54 pm	◐18 ☽→ ♎ 4:54 am	19 ☽ in ♎
Sun enters Cancer20 ☽ v/c 6:52 am ☽→ ♏ 7:58 am ☉→ ♋ 11:32 pm ♃ Jupiter Retrograde	Summer Solstice 21 ☽ in ♏	22 ☽ v/c 2:43 am ☽→ ♐ 8:55 am ☿ Mercury Direct 6:00pm	23 ☽ in ♐ v/c 10:09 pm	Full Moon ○24 ☽→ ♑ 9:05 am Full Moon 2:41 pm	25 ☽ in ♑ ♆ Neptune Retrograde	26 ☽ v/c 8:49am ☽→ ♒ 10:08 am
27 ☽ in ♒ ☽ v/c 3:07 pm	28 ☽→ ♓ 1:51pm	29 ☽ in ♓	30 ☽ in ♓ ☽ v/c 1:39 pm ☽→ ♈ 9:21 pm			July S M T W T F S 1 2 3 4 5 6 7 8 9 10 11 12 13 14 15 16 17 18 19 20 21 22 23 24 25 26 27 28 29 30 31

July

I nurture my inner Light with uplifting thoughts and connections.

July 2021

Sunday	Monday	Tuesday	Wednesday	Thursday	Friday	Saturday
June S M T W T F S 1 2 3 4 5 6 7 8 9 10 11 12 13 14 15 16 17 18 19 20 21 22 23 24 25 26 27 28 29 30				**1** ☽ in ♉	**2** ☽ v/c 12:15am	**3** ☽→♊ 8:28 am
4 ☽ in ♊	**5** ☽ in ♊ ☽ v/c 12:57pm ☽→♋ 9:24 pm	**6** ☽ in ♋	**7** ☽ v/c 12:20am	**8** ☽→♌ 9:51 am	New Moon ● **9** ☽ in ♌ New Moon 9:18 pm	**10** ☽ in ♌ ☽ v/c 12:10pm ☽→♍ 8:20 pm
11 ☽ in ♍	**12** ☽ v/c 8:29am	**13** ☽→♎ 4:30 am	**14** ☽ in ♎	**15** ☽ v/c 2:46am ☽→♏ 10:31 am	**16** ☽ in ♏	**17** ☽ v/c 7:03am ☽→♐ 2:38 pm
18 ☽ in ♐	**19** ☽ in ♐ ☽ v/c 12:30 pm ☽→♑ 5:08 pm	**20** ☽ in ♑	**21** ☽ in ♑ ☽ v/c 6:25pm ☽→♒ 6:36 pm	Sun Enters Leo **22** ☽ in ♒ ☉→♌ 10:26 am	Full Moon 10:38 ○ **23** ☽ in ♒ ☽ v/c 12:34pm ☽→♓ 8:12 pm	**24** ☽ in ♓
25 ☽ in ♓ ☽ v/c 7:14pm ☽→♈ 11:30 pm	**26** ☽ in ♈	**27** ☽ in ♈ ☽ v/c 9:13pm	**28** ☽→♉ 5:58 am	**29** ☽ in ♉	**30** ☽ in ♉ ☽ v/c 3:38pm ☽→♊ 4:08 pm	**31** ☽ in ♊ August S M T W T F S 1 2 3 4 5 6 7 8 9 10 11 12 13 14 15 16 17 18 19 20 21 22 23 24 25 26 27 28 29 30 31

August

My inner guidance, confidence and self-empowerment grows stronger with each new day.

August

Sunday	Monday	Tuesday	Wednesday	Thursday	Friday	Saturday
1 ☽ in ♉	2 ☽ v/c 3:41am ☽ -> ♊ 4:46 am	3 ☽ in ♊	4 ☽ in ♊ ☽ v/c 3:38pm ☽ -> ♋ 5:17 pm	5 ☽ in ♋	6 ☽ in ♋ ☽ v/c 6:12pm	7 ☽ -> ♌ 3:31 am
New Moon ● 8 ☽ in ♌ New Moon 9:51 am	9 ☽ v/c 8:23am ☽ -> ♍ 10:56 am	10 ☽ in ♍	11 ☽ v/c 7:22am ☽ -> ♎ 4:08 pm	12 ☽ in ♎	13 ☽ in ♎ ☽ v/c 4:39pm ☽ -> ♏ 8:01 pm	14 ☽ in ♏
◐ 15 ☽ in ♏ ☽ v/c 11:05pm ☽ -> ♐ 11:12 pm	16 ☽ in ♐	17 ☽ in ♐ ☽ v/c 9:43pm	18 ☽ -> ♑ 1:58 am	19 ☽ in ♑ ☽ v/c 7:59pm ♅ Uranus Retrograde	20 ☽ -> ♒ 4:49 am	21 ☽ in ♒
Full Moon 8:02am ○ 22 ☽ in ♒ ☽ v/c 8:02am ☽ -> ♓ 8:42 am ☉ -> ♍ 5:35 pm	23 ☽ in ♓	24 ☽ v/c 5:12am ☽ -> ♈ 2:57 pm	25 ☽ in ♈	26 ☽ in ♈ ☽ v/c 5:14pm	27 ☽ -> ♉ 12:27 am	28 ☽ in ♉
29 ☽ in ♉ ☽ v/c 10:58am ☽ -> ♊ 12:42 pm	◑ 30 ☽ in ♊	31 ☽ in ♊ ☽ v/c 4:48pm				

July

S	M	T	W	T	F	S
				1	2	3
4	5	6	7	8	9	10
11	12	13	14	15	16	17
18	19	20	21	22	23	24
25	26	27	28	29	30	31

September

S	M	T	W	T	F	S
			1	2	3	4
5	6	7	8	9	10	11
12	13	14	15	16	17	18
19	20	21	22	23	24	25
26	27	28	29	30		

September

September 2021

When I nurture and take care of myself, I become stronger and more balanced each day.

Sunday	Monday	Tuesday	Wednesday	Thursday	Friday	Saturday
August S M T W T F S 1 2 3 4 5 6 7 8 9 10 11 12 13 14 15 16 17 18 19 20 21 22 23 24 25 26 27 28 29 30 31			**1** ☽☽→ ⟐ 1:26 am	**2** ☽ in ⟐	**3** ☽ v/c 1:37am ☽→ ⟐ 11:58 am	**4** ☽ in ⟐
5 ☽ in ⟐ ☽ v/c 10:22am ☽→ ⟐ 7:06pm	**New Moon ● 6** ☽ in ⟐ New Moon 8:53 pm Rosh Hashanah Labor Day	**7** ☽ in ⟐ ☽ v/c 3:24pm ☽→ ⟐ 11:20 pm	**8** ☽ in ⟐	**9** ☽ v/c 12:48am ☽→ ⟐ 2:05 am	**10**	**11** ☽ in ⟐
Grandparents Day 12 ☽ v/c 1:33am ☽→ ⟐ 4:34 am	**◗ 13** ☽ in ⟐	**14** ☽ v/c 6:57am ☽→ ⟐ 7:34 am	**Yom Kippur 15** ☽ in ⟐	**16** ☽ v/c 1:40am ☽→ ⟐ 11:23 am	**17** ☽ in ⟐	**18** ☽ v/c 5:14am ☽→ ⟐ 4:22 pm
19 ☽ in ⟐	**Full Moon ○ 20** ☽ in ⟐ Full Moon 4:19 am ☽ v/c 7:56pm ☽→ ⟐ 11:13 pm	**21** ☽ in ⟐	**Sun Enters Libra 22** ☽ in ⟐ ☽ v/c 10:05pm ☉→ ⟐ 3:21 pm Autumn Equinox	**23** ☽→ ⟐ 8:38am	**24** ☽ in ⟐	**25** ☽ v/c 9:09am ☽→ ⟐ 8:36 pm
26 ☽ in ⟐	**27** ☽ in ⟐ ☿ Mercury Retrograde 1:10 am	**28** ☽ v/c 12:18am ☽→ ⟐ 9:34 am	**29** ☽ in ⟐	**30** ☽ in ⟐ ☽ v/c 10:48am ☽→ ⟐ 8:53 pm		**October** S M T W T F S 1 2 3 4 5 6 7 8 9 10 11 12 13 14 15 16 17 18 19 20 21 22 23 24 25 26 27 28 29 30 31

October

I open my heart and listen, allowing my inner guidance to show me the way.

October 2021

Sunday	Monday	Tuesday	Wednesday	Thursday	Friday	Saturday
September S M T W T F S 1 2 3 4 5 6 7 8 9 10 11 12 13 14 15 16 17 18 19 20 21 22 23 24 25 26 27 28 29 30					World Vegetarian Day 1 ☽ in ♌	2 ☽ in ♌ ☽ v/c 7:43 pm
3 ☽→ ♍ 4:38 am	4 ☽ in ♍	5 ☽ v/c 4:46 am ☽→ ♎ 8:41 am	New Moon ● 6 ☽ in ♎ New Moon 7:06 am ♇ Pluto Direct	7 ☽ v/c 1:03am ☽→ ♏ 10:22 am	8 ☽ in ♏	9 ☽ v/c 2:05am ☽→ ♐ 11:24 am
10 ☽ in ♐ ♄ Saturn Direct	11 ☽ v/c 12:30am ☽→ ♑ 1:15 pm	12 ☽ in ♑	◐ 13 ☽ v/c 6:53 am ☽→ ♒ 4:47 pm	14 ☽ in ♒	15 ☽ v/c 8:33 am ☽→ ♓ 10:22 pm	16 ☽ in ♓
17 ☽ in ♓ ☽ v/c 7:24 pm	18 ☽→ ♈ 6:04 am ♃ Jupiter Direct ☿ Mercury Direct 11:17am	19 ☽ in ♈	Full Moon ○ 20 ☽ in ♈ Full Moon 10:56 am ☽ v/c 10:56 am ☽→ ♉ 3:59 pm	21 ☽ in ♉	22 ☽ in ♉ ☽ v/c 4:35 pm	Sun Enters Scorpio 23 ☽→ ♊ 3:57 am ☉→ ♏ 12:51am
24 ☽ in ♊	25 ☽ in ♊ ☽ v/c 10:11 am ☽→ ♋ 5:00 pm	26 ☽ in ♋	27 ☽ in ♋	◑ 28 ☽ v/c 2:02 am ☽→ ♌ 5:07 am	29 ☽ in ♌	30 ☽ v/c 3:05 am ☽→ ♍ 2:09 pm
☽ in ♍ Halloween 31						November S M T W T F S 1 2 3 4 5 6 7 8 9 10 11 12 13 14 15 16 17 18 19 20 21 22 23 24 25 26 27 28 29 30

November

As I break free of limiting ways of being, as my life opens and expands in amazing ways.

November 2021

Sunday	Monday	Tuesday	Wednesday	Thursday	Friday	Saturday
October S M T W T F S 1 2 3 4 5 6 7 8 9 10 11 12 13 14 15 16 17 18 19 20 21 22 23 24 25 26 27 28 29 30 31	**1** ☽ in ♏︎ ☽ v/c 1:00 pm ☽→ ♎︎ 7:11 pm	**Election Day 2** ☽ in ♎︎	**3** ☽ in ♎︎ ☽ v/c 6:32 pm ☽→ ♏︎ 8:52 pm	**New Moon ● 4** ☽ in ♏︎ New Moon 5:16 pm	**5** ☽ in ♏︎ ☽ v/c 12:10 pm ☽→ ♐︎ 8:52 pm	**6** ☽ in ♐︎
D S ◐ End 7 ☽ v/c 8:44 am ☽→ ♑︎ 8:03 pm	**8** ☽ in ♑︎	**9** ☽ in ♑︎ ☽ v/c 12:51 pm ☽→ ♒︎ 10:03 pm	**10** ☽ in ♒︎	**Veterans Day 11** ☽ in ♒︎ ☽ v/c 2:52 pm	**12** ☽→ ♓︎ 2:53 am	**13** ☽ in ♓︎
14 ☽ v/c 12:40 am ☽→ ♈︎ 10:48 am	**15** ☽ in ♈︎	**16** ☽ in ♈︎ ☽ v/c 10:51 am ☽→ ♉︎ 9:18 pm	**17** ☽ in ♉︎	**18** ☽ in ♉︎	**Full Moon ○ 19** Lunar Eclipse 3:59am ☽ in ♉︎ ☽ v/c 3:57 am ☽→ ♊︎ 9:33 am	**20** ☽ in ♊︎
Sun Enters Sagittarius 21 ☽ in ♊︎ ☽ v/c 10:52 am ☽→ ♋︎ 10:33 pm ☉→ ♐︎ 10:33 am	**22** ☽ in ♋︎	**23** ☽ in ♋︎	**24** ☽ v/c 12:02 am ☽→ ♌︎ 10:58 am	**Thanksgiving Day 25** ☽ in ♌︎	**26** ☽ in ♌︎ ☽ v/c 11:24 am ☽→ ♍︎ 9:12 pm	**☽ 27** ☽ in ♍︎
Hanukkah Begins 28 ☽ in ♍︎ ☽ v/c 7:02 pm	**29** ☽→ ♎︎ 3:55 am	**30** ☽ in ♎︎ ☽ v/c 11:19 pm				**December** S M T W T F S 1 2 3 4 5 6 7 8 9 10 11 12 13 14 15 16 17 18 19 20 21 22 23 24 25 26 27 28 29 30 31

December

Peace and serenity fill and surround me.

December 2021

Sunday	Monday	Tuesday	Wednesday	Thursday	Friday	Saturday
(November)			1 ☽→♏ 6:55pm ♆ Neptune Direct	2 ☽ in ♏	3 ☽ v/c 12:22 am ☽→♐ 7:13am	New Moon ● 4 Solar Eclipse 2:44 am ☽ in ♐
5 ☽ v/c 12:08 am ☽→♑ 6:31am	6 ☽ in ♑ ☽ v/c 11:42 pm	Pearl Harbor Day 7 ☽→♒ 6:48am	8 ☽ in ♒	9 ☽ v/c 4:59 am ☽→♓ 9:53am	10 ☽ in ♓	◐ 11 ☽ in ♓ ☽ v/c 2:40 pm ☽→♈ 4:46pm
12 ☽ in ♈	13 ☽ in ♈ ☽ v/c 9:52 pm	14 ☽→♉ 3:11am	15 ☽ in ♉	16 ☽ in ♉ ☽ v/c 11:08 am ☽→♊ 3:43pm	17 ☽ in ♊	Full Moon ○ 18 ☽ in ♊ Full Moon 7:42 pm
19 v/c 1:02 am ☽→♋ 4:42am ♀ Venus Retrograde	20 ☽ in ♋	Winter Solstice 21 ☽ v/c 9:44 am ☽→♌ 4:54pm ☉→♑ 10:59am Sun enters Capricorn	22 ☽ in ♌	23 ☽ in ♌	24 ☽ v/c 1:39 am ☽→♍ 3:24am	Christmas Day 25 ☽ in ♍
26 v/c 3:40 am ☽→♎ 11:24am	◑ 27 ☽ in ♎	28 ☽ v/c 4:11 pm ☽→♏ 4:16pm	29 ☽ in ♏	30 ☽ in ♏ ☽ v/c 12:10 pm ☽→♐ 6:08 pm	31 ☽ in ♐ ☽ v/c 3:00 pm	(January)

November

S	M	T	W	T	F	S
	1	2	3	4	5	6
7	8	9	10	11	12	13
14	15	16	17	18	19	20
21	22	23	24	25	26	27
28	29	30				

January

S	M	T	W	T	F	S
						1
2	3	4	5	6	7	8
9	10	11	12	13	14	15
16	17	18	19	20	21	22
23	24	25	26	27	28	29
30	31					

www.ingramcontent.com/pod-product-compliance
Lightning Source LLC
LaVergne TN
LVHW072101070426

835508LV00002B/208